WHAT WAS I THINKING

?

Ziji
PUBLISHING

WHAT WAS I THINKING

Collection 1995 – 2018

JAFFAR KHAN

Copyright © Jaffar Khan 2018

The right of Jaffar Khan to be identified as the author of this work has been asserted in accordance with sections 77 and 78 of the Copyright, Designs and Patents Act 1988

All rights reserved. No part of this publication may be reproduced, stored in a retrieval system, or transmitted in any form or by any means, electronic, mechanical, photocopying, recording, or otherwise, without the prior permission of both the copyright owner and the below publisher of this book.

Published by Ziji Publishing Ltd. In 2018
www.zijipublishing.com

Distributed by Turnaround Distribution Services Ltd
www.turnaround-uk.com
Telephone 0208829 3000

ISBN: 978-1-908628-14-5

Printed and bound in Great Britain by Aquatint Ltd

For:

Suzanne, Zayn and Kamil

A promise kept

There is a Djinn / in my tonic

A shape shifting / ironic fellow

Dressed in a cloak of flames

Smiling / all the while

Waiting to make a deal

jk

CONTENTS

I

Dawn	1
Habana Bay	2
Mount Rundle	3
Calgary	4
Merida Evening	5
An Ancient Language	6
Light	8
Old Woman	9
The Convergence	10
Spring	12
Frida Kahlo	13
Mexico City	16
Bad Moon	17
Feudals In Heaven	20
Paranoia	22
Brujas In The Bushes	23

II

Anthropologist	29
Astral	30
Cosmic Spiral	31
The River Myth	32
Avalon Fading	34
Rule	35
Skies	36
Intersection	37
Symbols	38
Life Force	39

III

The Changeling (a dream)	43
Visiting Angel	45
Ready	46
The Inevitable	47
Life Tree	48
Ode To Nina Simone	49

Beautiful Liars	50
Dragonfly	52
Somewhere In Thailand	53
The Quality Of Things	54
Naked Sands	55
Millennium Prayer	56
Racing Pigeons	57

IV

Flood And The Drought	61
Drones Over Hindu Kush	63
The Offer	64
Eternal Recurrence	65
Confederacy Of Liars	66
Whirling	68
Karachi Wedding	69
Lahore Playground	70
Sectarian Times	71

V

The Theft	75
A Dead Poet	76
Invisible Things	77
Creators	78
Ode To My Mother	79
The Cave	81
A Special Case	83
A Rural Evening	85
The Dialectic	86
Welcome To The World	88
The Announcement	90
The Metaphysical God	91
The Gift	93
Postcard To My Son	95
The Witness	96

I

Dawn

Men slake their thirst
At the dawn of meaning
Like animals lapping
At the edge of a shimmering lake

We reap our sorrows
And we harvest our joys
In mid-stream we awake
From moment to moment
Like drunk drivers in traffic

Oh hello officer, tell me
Was I just born?
Or did I just die over there?

Havana Bay

Like summer's scent
The sound of a distant bell
Floats carefree
Upon these coastal breezes

Upon some eternal shores
Angels are on sentinel duty
They are on the look out
For a lone man's journey

Mount Rundle

Is that you / looking upon the world
Is that you / calling
Across gossamer veil
Covering the fissures of self?

And these imprints upon
The filament of being
Are they stories of other lifetimes?
Hand prints in an ancient cave?

Hues of the self / dissolving / re-forming
Shimmer in the numinous air

A shudder hole opens
In the fabric of space
A mountain disappears!

A mythic wind blows
Across the valley
Rumours of worlds unborn
Worlds unstrung / an insistent call
To transcendent beginnings

Trees whisper news / of the moment

Calgary

    Windswept snow
    Diffusion
        of lamplight
    Radiant crystals on hedges…

    Who would have thought
    That this was once
        a city

Merida Evening

A black bat
in darkening sky
swirls
      swoops
wings that whisper …

A life plucked
from the night-blue water

A firefly
floats indifferently
its tiny beacon - symbol
of tangential journeys

A floating memory
of childhood courtyards…

Next door
the German shepherd
incis-ively
tears up the tropical night

An Ancient Language

Waves of sentient light
Veins of light and dark
Traverse below the skein of this Earth
This perfect revelation!

Hooked by dreams of the real
The world once again
Dreams itself a brand new dislocation
No longer does the wind carry
History's voices and whispers and stories:
And no longer do we and
Trees and animals and rivers
Speak the common language of life

Witnesses only to our selves
We no longer sense the solar wings
That open and close like a butterfly's…

Push-pull actors drunk with dreams
In a no-yes drama
Trichotomies of flame we are
A hunger so deep for self we become
The songs of pleasure and pain…

Needle sharing addicts - brothers to the skin
Toreros with bandoleers!
Pinned by tin horns we still scorch the wind
With our dreams of glory

Virtual sons of mind we are
Searching the killing fields
for the great mandala of Being

Homeless and clamorous
This gathering of souls –
This leakage of light in fissures of rock
This collective dreaming –
…….this shadow play of God

And in the dream world
Where we make ourselves
Spirit shakes with laughter
Bathes the blue-blue world
With the cool-cool ray of Being

For God sake
Bring back the arcing sky
For another banner try!

Light

This sudden
        spectral light
from your eyes

reminds me
        of spilled crystals
upon naked sands.

There is more
        to this light
than meets the eye

Old Woman

      The old woman kneeling
In the dim recesses of archways
A figure shrouded in devotion
She has been kneeling forever –

A saint
Caught in shards of coloured light
The face of prayer she.....

I come often to watch her pray
And her ancient face – lit by a single candle
Etched deeply by the lines of her life

And I sit there quietly to let
her compassion wash over me

God's own creator she…

The Convergence

Travelers then - we are still
Our lives shifting and sliding
The ebb and flow of a mighty tide
Even at rest you cannot fix
The location of anything but
The orphan heart

Comrades then upon the path:
Points of no return we met
Upon trajectories that converged
In a city that exists within a city
A convergence nobody imagined
From different corners we came
And reaching behind the mirror
Of a thousand shifting faces
Counterfeits we tried to reclaim

Wayfarers then - we are still
Upon unchartered pathways
Our bodies are warm continents
Molten streams below the crust
Diaphanous the heart.......

We are older now - yet still not done
Here resting by some road-side
Our minds are like unchained electrons:
Brief words float unfettered
Like midsummer balloons against
A sky of silence
The very silence
That cradles the core of things.

Spring

Long months of submergence -
    this tiny pulse
        below an icy skein

Born again – it is carving
    its playful way
        emerald through whiteness

Jewelled pebbles -
Stones of precious time
    turning my mind
        toward a different world

Frida Kahlo

Her *Casa Azul* in Coyoacan:
A time capsule of a life - the life of art and politics
A life of spiralling pain…
And watched over by Marx and Lenin and Stalin
The trinity of her political gods
She yet floated above her bed
Just like the paper-Mache creations
Of Diego Rivera her companion star

And like his murals and sculptures she
Came from a place deep within the soul
Of this ancient of lands - a soul
Trampled by the hoofs of the conquistador:
His gleaming armour reflecting
The gaping horror of surprise -
His dumb rage impregnating the fertile land

Oh the wave upon wave of visitation!
They came - the bureaucrats of Christ
Casting the snares of domesticity -
And then the unrelenting train
Of the skull-capped inquisition
To squeeze the last drop of errant blood - until
Even the clarity of pain was impossible.

And in the deep place of the soul
An ancient psychic formulation
Accepted it and still accepts it all.

Her face
An unsmiling determination
Behind those large luminous eyes
Proud and dark and mysterious
Heavy eyebrows - an ominous thunderstorm
Contained by unseen bands of light and dark
She of the formidable will - formed
In a regal acceptance of pain and of death
A child of mystery she gave birth
To the Azteca mystery

Frida - how fame becomes you:
Self- portraits etched by a disembodied eye
Now fill bookstores and museums
Frida - you laughed but never before the mirror
The mirror which was with you always
Even while you lay in the canopied bed
And painted Frida with a necklace of thorns

Frida as an antlered deer stuck with arrows
Frida in strips of white binding
……the naked body sundered
By the cracked central column of her being
Frida with the mandala of death
And another Frida
With a picture of her Diego - glowing
In the centre of her forehead:
Frida - pinned by nails she bled white tears.

And now a ghost walks the house
Observing the concretions of a life:
Beads necklaces stones and rings
The dresses - the kitchen - her collection.
......a wheel chair in a sunny room
Beside which lie the painter's tools
An easel with an unfinished portrait…
Frida's painted body-caste
Now abandoned - upon the empty bed

      And over the years
Without Frida's colours - her spirit
All the stone gods in the garden
Have lost their composure

Mexico City

Along Vito Alessio Robles
The tall jacarandas bloom
A violet earth…

Abandoned small boots
        Lie lace-less
Under the concrete boulevard bench

I watch a nameless family
Bundled with firewood
Like explorers making their way
Against a hard cold north wind

Bundled children these
Precious little satellites….
Orbit the mother's flowing skirt

Skipping their way
To the night shelter
Below the concrete highways
They light a small fire
To eat small beans
To think great ideas

Below the roaring rapids
        of the great city

Bad Moon

Tonight a rare bad moon hangs
Over the Bay of Havana
Desultory lovers on the Malecón
They cling to each other and their bicycles
All the way from fraternal China

Deep in Habana Vieja – once fabled jewel
Now a crumbling heritage
A matted dusty *bichon havanese*
Follows morosely at the heels
Of the woman dressed in red
She is in motion - the caramel mulata
The Ivory Coast imprisoned in sway of her hips
She has been liberated by spandex….

Not for her the chains of the new world!
She has the immunity of the dark glide
Drawn by the pendent night - hers
Are the dreams of the innocent – she swings
Past revolutionary murals
Upon walls of faded paint hanging wires
There an indignant Fidel - his eyes
Upon a universal horizon
And there the martyred Ché
The star of the struggle upon the famous beret

The revolutionary soliloquy submerged
Under radiation of orbiting satellites

Red high heels upon gutted sidewalk
She floats upon some airy strata
Past the famed Floridita -
Where once Papa Hemingway anointed
The perfect daiquiri – proclaiming:
This is my favourite time and place!

The tribes of Habana Vieja are gathering
At the Hemingway Marina (*our Ernest honoured again*)
To dance with leg-tied European tourists
They drink the heady moonlight - inhale
The hot-trucking-rhythm of afro salsa
And the girls are like exclamations!
Sparking across the floor….
This is a community of pelvic frenzy
A near tropical fever of pride
A poppy-field of glistening skins
Droplets from a common destiny
The full moon is closer still
A remorseless cold shining it is

The music: a unique weave of rhythms
It's a transfusion of heart-beats
As the horn players let loose dipping and turning
The sequined elegance of their moves
An answer to lunar tyranny

Under the brazen stare of the moon
Time and polemic is suspended
The dancers raise an orgasmic war cry
Like sails upon a windless sea -

And the rare bad moon begins to blush

Feudals In Heaven

Living as a feudal
In a socialist land -
The guard at my gate has
Broken knuckles and
His elbows re-arranged.
His arm is not an arm
It is a weapon with range

Living as a feudal in
A socialist land -
The maid thinks she's Japanese -
Brings us 'red rose' tea
      on bended knees
And just when I think
I have figured out this place
A woman tries a death leap
Across my car on an empty street
The image of desperate eyes
Still imprinted upon my mind

"Socialismo o Muerte!" taken too far

    And in the eyes
Of the *Commandante* trails
The smoke of uncertainty
For never did he believe
He would come this way
To a cuffed destiny

But he is the *Commandante*
Chosen by the spirits
A feudal by any other name
In a socialist land

Paranoia

The mics looks like a spiders
The web is a clever device -
Outside the slatted window
There is somebody moving
Counting my breathing
Taking the measure of a life

And who is that breathing
In the corner of the bedroom
Was that a gurgling laugh?
And this stab of pain - in
The lower-lower back
Is this a medical condition - or
A needle in the stack

And outside the garden
The tropical birds are chattering
Reporting details of our embraces
To the man raking the garden

Brujas In The Bushes*

        A dangerous location - to be stationary
On this stretch of *Cinta Avendida*
For there are *brujas* lurking in the bushes
        Renowned for their speed and stealth
And as the enchantment of the Sufi poetry
Electrifies the Havana night - carried
Upon Nusrat Fateh Ali's vocal acrobatics
        (a strange musical juxtaposition in the land
        of salsa and afro jazz)
A hair-raising vibe whips my neck around
And there she is! – a *bruja* in my Lada!
Slipped in without me hearing *nada*
And when I eject her with choice words
She slides out heels first - demanding
Oye, donde va!
A mi gusta mucho la musica!

I make my way up a fragmented house
Mesmeric sounds of *santeria* drums
Fill the darkened hallways and rooms
The building is teeming with invited djinns
Happily in possession of the older denizens
Twisting them into strange animistic forms
The djinns are having a good laugh
While spraying mouthfuls of rum in the air

At the roof top - two *santeria* priests - busy
With incantations and dispensing powders
No doubt of attraction and repulsion
And passing around a bottle of *siete años*
They call for a sacrifice to *Orula* - lord of divination
And with solemn ritual - a throat is slit
 A pigeon dies – white feathers float
Against the glow of the *Capitolio* dome…
        And somewhere - Colonel Alberto Ortero
Fidel's omniscient director of security
Suffers sharp stabs of depression - crying
Que coño, POR QUE?

Rosario is a seer - a high priestess of *Yoruba*
With eyes that see a thousand miles
She talks to the dead above my head
And dressed in the white of an initiate
She smokes a cohiba 'esplendida'
And every so often interrupts her dialogue
With the other world – she commands:
Pass me the fuego mi amor!

Driving home through a drama of
A lightening riven cloudscape
Miles Davis is in the seat playing -
The tonal clarity of his legendary trumpet
Colliding with the ocean spray
And of course *Papi* Marx is looking down
Surely - from a dialectical heaven
As I contemplate the idea of
A single pure note
Transforming the world

On a night like this - everything is possible

*Bruja – (Bru-ha) : meaning 'witch' a term used commonly in Cuba.

II

Anthropologist

In these dappled high woods
There is a circulation of geometries:
Like a Druid amongst the stags
His shadow slips away to dance
      to a wilder tune

Where once the rule of blood
Now flow ancient dreams
The most ancient of sounds
Race the highways of the heart

Where once lurked thought
A question - a promise……wild eyes now
Freeze in the floodlight of time:

Cities fall to rise again
Imprints of life forgotten
In his palm there are innuendos
Of life hidden

Sun spiked particles circling….
Must be the dust of millenniums

Astral

Eyes can also hear!
You touch me - colours collide
Your smile - a river of tears
Your pain a window to galaxies

Inside out and outside in
Skin absorbs the folds of night
Time's great circle is a step taken
To the very beginning

Perfidious tongue !
Hold to silence
As a lover - to an embrace

For all is fluidity
Coalescence and linkage
Insubstantial this world
A careening wild horse
An astral choking

Flames of the desire body
Burning
Burning the earth's body

Cosmic Spiral

Time squeezed
Space expanded
Space spiralled
To a point where
Time vanished

These things happen

The point of arrival
Moment of departure
Do we truly know -
Only by hear-say

Can you recall
First sight
First quest(ion)
First love first insight
What is out and what inside?

The River Myth

They still speak of a great river
Old as the ancient of days
New as a baby's first kick
As a quantum of now it flows
And flows -
It's place of ending a rumour
Whispered by blind prophets

Some currents are as swift
As the speed of thought
Strong as the wheels of desire
Some eddies stall you by some shady bank
Where you dream of journeys end

Lifetimes pass in its whirlpools.

But the river is complex
....no simple outing this
Its sources infinite....
It contains all in its path:
The hum of the universe
The spiral of the galaxy
Fire of the solar system
Loneliness of angels...
The night and day of earth
Night stirrings of animals
Trembling of continents
The fury of our nations and cultures
The sound of races on the march

On its endless meandering journey
The great river gathers into its current
Old newspapers broken toys new cars
From our streets and towns
It embraces wholesale the lives
Of friends and their friends
Wives children parents brothers and sisters
It loves to devour our dreams and visions.

It will drown you in a second.

Avalon Fading.....

The sound of crickets I remember
In fields spilled with silver moonlight
Quail wings like rapid heart-beats
Drumming through shafts of golden wheat

A beam of light piercing an empty room
I remember the clink of glasses between friends
Whose shadows were also friends.....

You and I have danced all night
Stepping into strange rooms
Through unmarked portals
Which were not there before
And weren't there after

So tell me what happened
To the children running and playing
In the alleys and bazaars
Of a world that has all but faded

The occidental and oriental mythologies
Are now drifting away
It is autumn.

Rule

In this
I am not a pro
but I would think:

To dedicate one's life
to the rule
of Love

Now THAT
would be something
to write home about

Skies

For some the sky is ruthless ice
For some an expression of infinity:
>   interlocking spheres
>   parallel realities.
For some a battleground of deities
>   a clash of mythologies
>   a collision of heaven and earth.
For some - a curtain of compassion.

Some see their dreams in clouds...
Some see the dome of oppression:
>   preordained
>   webbing of fate
It rains beauty for some - for some
>   rain clouds of knowing
>   meteors of transformation,
Others are struck dumb - cowering
>   in mists of unknowing.
For some spirits ride great white stallions
>   blazing sunsets are scriptures
>   jagged parapets of belief..

Others go about their business
Counting blades of grass......

The Intersection

Man stands at the intersection
A home for hungry energies
Time / like a swarm of bees
Pollinating a field of wild flowers

On his right:
Division and endless subdivision
Particles devolving into waves
On his left:
Infinity of zeroes - domains
Each a microcosm to the other

Waves emerging as particles

Symbols

A grain of sand embedded
in the stuff of truth......

From the forest of language
we pluck offerings - we wave
simulacrums of reality

Like red banners atop
abandoned alters - stained temples:
Untended gateways

to the great black stone
of mystery.

Life force

It dances in spirit freelance
It mutates in seeds of change
It spirals in quantum flowers
Flowers as the truth of matter

It rages it howls it hoops it loops

It sputters in urban gutters
In titles of hope it prints
Insisting in the march of roots
It presses hard upon
The wombs of fecundity

It whistles it skips it hollers
Through the porticos of mystery
Like a carefree schoolboy
On an outing

III

The Changeling (a dream)

It is an ordinary day
        an ordinary view
Instant by fearful instant
I become aware that I am
Rapidly losing sight:

The world turns opaque
A milky film across jaded eyes
No panic yet:
That's cool I thought to be blind
Might have possibilities
(ask a blind man that)

Then quickly the dim world
Darkens to black
Increasing asphyxiation -
The air is becoming poison
No longer mine this world
Panic choking struggle
Out of my element
To the waterside I run
Gasping and surely dying

But then there is the deep blue
Inviting calling to me
It is mine this water
And choking - on the edge of death
I take a leap of faith

A brief moment of struggle
A gasping - a drowning
A surrender to my fate
Then a deep inhalation
And life returning in great gulps

A revelation:
This is my element now
I am a new aquatic species
With light in my head
Free joyous in a vast ocean

Only to become aware of
The circling sharks

Visiting Angel

For some years I could barely see
But for a jar from the highlands
A pipe-full of God's herb
I could barely…love

But then:
All thanks to a nameless visiting angel
Disguised cunningly as my dog *Mosie*
Hand me a glass of the simple stuff
Even from the lowlands give me
A hint a gesture the word
Will I then show you
The flame of initiation
Which I protect
From howling winds
In the sanctity of a small cave

Ready

    Majestic leaves sale
            upon the wind
    Eddies of flight -
    An ordained immersion

    Open to the Eye of the Buddha
    I too am ready:

    Sails unfurled and bows drawn
    Upon the ocean of *Tao*

    Poised on the border of
    This world and the non-manifest

    I can only offer silence

The Inevitable

He told himself
Yes...well
It's not too late -
Let us cauterize the arteries of desire
Let us expel
        the little engines of karma -

And why not

Look around you
The impossible
        is here

The inevitable
        is lurking
Just over your shoulder

Life Tree

The life tree grows
Year by year – imbibing
Our actions and reactions
Without remorse
Feeding the roots of expectation
A metaphor-creating reality
Branching to a reality-creating metaphor
Ad-infinitum!

A spiralling endless branching

Ode To Nina Simone

Nina, you sang to us of lonely roads
Your off-key passion gave us hope
You struck a blow for compassion
You struck the bells of destitution
As you looked out at the audience
With your fearless fuck-you gaze
Not a sign of appeasement in your eyes

Nina, we fell for you in our bed-sits
We fell for you in London jazz clubs
We fell for the songs of exile
You sang the blues of another kind
You sang the tunes of ethereal loss

And then when you did that swing
When you did that rolling rock
Ah your voice shook the timbers
Of our young unfettered souls
So - like leaves clinging to a tree
We were clinging tight to each other
During those wild midnight hours

Nina it seems we have known you forever.

Beautiful Liars:

They were napalmed in Vietnam
While working- behind enemy lines
They discussed future economic policy
With Chairman Deng Xiaoping - while strolling
Along the Great Wall of China
They swung through the girders of the Eiffel Tower
One by one - low fruit in the Parisian night…
In Windsor Castle - they took high tea
With Her Majesty Queen Elizabeth
And in the back alleys of Cairo - they supped
With baleful *djinns* - who left them no quarter
They drove the hazardous ice-highways of the North
Their paintings hang in the Prado
In between Velasquez and Picasso

Now this band of septuagenarians
Is gathered - in a suburban basement
To compete in the world poker finals
Between them - not a word passes
For each man guards - the winning hand
And before they can call each other
Digby stands up - to make a confession:

WHAT WAS I THINKING? JAFFAR KHAN

All these years you believed I was CIA
Working undercover as an accountant
In fact - I have always been a poet –
Yes a poet - a secret I kept from you
But now I am letting you know this – in case
We don't make it back – from Mount K2

To a man - the gang of beautiful liars
Stands up - dropping their winning hands
They haul Digby out - into the back alley
And they beat him about the head – with sticks
And as they hobble down the dim alley
Digby slumped against the garbage bins
He shouts at them - through a bleeding mouth

I finally got one over you – ya' bastards!

Dragonfly

I would be quite content
but for that crazy dragonfly's
incandescent flight
        to who knows where

Yesterday
our paths crossed again –
it thrummed around my head
as I sat upon the porch

Powered by warp drive
it emerged out of nothing
right in front of my face
and scanned every inch of me
mocking me with its absolute
stillness
and then it vanished!

 I swear it's passing
        cast a shadow upon the sun.

We are not poor moths
fluttering towards the light
we are embedded in light itself

And existence
what did you say it was?

Somewhere in Thailand…

Every morning
some birds
sing outside my window
in a language
        I cannot know

I hear glass marbles
tumbling
        endlessly!

Back-to-back
surrounded by a thousand
smiling buddhas

We make our last stand

Quality Of Things

Everything that emerges into existence
Human animal plant flower mineral
Brings with it an ineffable quality
Its very own signature as an individual thing
It is something that lies behind and beyond
Colour scent shape and size
Its projection is a shout into the world

"There is more to me than you can see"

Take the case of the plant named 'Indigo'
Did the elders sit down one day and decide:
"The colour of this flower is to be called Indigo"
Or did the plant announce itself
Stamped itself upon the human tongue
Murmuring quietly to the woman
As she gathered her roots and seeds

"Hey hey my name is Indigo!"

Does not Beauty speak for itself?

Naked Sands

This sudden
        spectral light
from your eyes

Reminds me
        of spilled crystals
upon naked sands

When the sun shines
I am blinded
        by images

In the dark
I go hunting
        like a fruit-bat

Millennium Prayer

Salutations to the rising sun!
Here's to the new millennium sky!
May the pestilential hand of humanity
Get zapped and smoked and charred
Let a new connectivity is my prayer
Bolt across this spinning globe

But whose millennium is it you ask
Fidel Castro denies all knowledge
Papuans under shrinking canopies
Are reflecting upon their gourds:
"Fill 'em boys with the best wine
let us drink and see some visions!"

In the canyons of these vertical cities
The circus of the absurd is on a roll
And we pray for that remote control
That will freeze once and forever the
Consuming maw of the man-machine
That never stops to question why
      Only how

Yes friends the new millennium is upon us
And from all directions upending forces
Are converging

Ready to score an early goal

Racing Pigeons

As children we took delight
Watching the world from our roof-top:

The great wheeling flights
       of white racing pigeons
Winged our fancy dreams

Now the dreams have all
       come home to roost -

One by one they peel the colours
       from the once limitless skies

In a world without signs
       we await new orders

IV

Flood And The Drought

When the hot wind howls, which it surely will
And when empty buckets are filled with sand
Men will run for cover across this Indus land
Now everyone's lips are parched with news
Of a great wave sighted on the horizon
Its either flood or drought on this ancient land

I have been away so long I can never come back

Glaciers are receding sea levels rising
The Empires they are in aggressive denial
Some because they have too much
The others they can never have enough
Nations are beggars wanting to be tigers
Deadly toys in abundance in the factories of promise
They are working to rule in the factories of peace
To the merchants of the dark iron
A stone thrown is a delightful garland of beads
But who cares after all - it's all an experiment
Good news - our spermatozoa are mutating
Every ejaculation pleases our merciful God
The good and evil of it - the beauty and the despair
You might say: *'Do not dance alone boys and gals*
God will be mighty pissed'

Time is a figure eight you might discover
Universes are strung out to kingdom come
Go in through that hole at the centre of our galaxy
And you may never come this way again
But you know all about that kind of magic
That knowledge lies at the core of our being

Mustard flowers upon a blazing field

And the proverbial man teetering above the abyss
He thinks he is strolling through a rose garden
They are everywhere men like that
You try to warn them, grab their sleeve
They look at you and laugh their heads off

I am pressured by the cycle of events
I am weighed down by history
I am weighed down by beauty
Mine and yours and everyone's
And thinking of this I go and sit under the mango tree
To watch the dark hours coalesce
      around the bright stars

Luminous ghosts move through the orchard.

Drones Over Hindu Kush

Spy v. spy in the streets of Lahore
Uncle Sam's drones above the Hindu Kush
Taliban drones exploding vests of nails
Media drones spreading lies on screens
Political drones cowering in leather chairs
Tribal drones bombing empty schools
Bearded drones killing women for honour
Fundo drones spraying spittle of hate
Liberal drones locking up the gates
Gangland drones locked on multi targets
MBA drones locked on Ivy League schools
Urban drones sipping scotch and water
Feudal drones scratching their balls
Sufi drones running to Canada…

How many drones a nation make?

The Offer

Well, he had said his nostrums
Laid out lines along certain axis
The traps were secure - the nets were out
Prayers had been said and
Djinns invoked on his behalf
At what price no one cared to ask

A powerful talisman hung around his neck

Sure enough the invocations delivered:
One day the job offer arrived like a
Slingshot through the front door
And it lay there upon the marble floor
A pulsating insistent creature
From an unwelcome world

Good fortune! Shouted his friends
Celebrating raucously well into dawn
The lucky man sensing doom
Dove under the bed covers shaking:
Willing the world and the postman
To move on down the street
To another door

Eternal Recurrence

You keep returning to this room
Looking for the remains of the banquet
Long after the table has been picked
Yet you keep on turning the door handle

Long after the red sun has set
You cover your eyes with dark glasses
The rain clouds are spent now, drained
Yet you walk with a black umbrella

Your black dog running by your side
Has now taken to carrying a white cane

Long since you jettisoned
Wrinkled bits and pieces of yourself
You continued to fill the empty jar
With those old wines that long ago
Turned to crimson acid

Red and yellow rose vines -
They are the walls of your prison
Be careful of the sharp thorns
As you contemplate their beauty

Confederacy Of Liars

We are the somnolent guests
At a beggars banquet -
This caravan of bankruptcy
These wayward banners of nationalism
These faux proud men with their beards
Men with their khaki fatigues and dark suits
Not a soul of honour in sight

It's the oldest game on Earth
Martyrdom is what's needed
For the tribe and the greater good
The miasma of evil is spreading
Be ready to kill to save the world
Honour your god - bomb and maim away
Civilization needs a homogenized populace
The imperatives of war – the progress of science
Gather power - for it is manifest destiny

And at all cost save the natives – from themselves
And there is not enough to go around
So grab it fast before the barbarians
Break down the city gates and take it all

They have been at it since time immemorial
Shaping and carving the destiny of nations
It is the doctrine of necessity
They have their cellars stocked with ballistic missiles
And their silos with vintage wines
That's how it is done – with a sleight of hand
Ponzi schemes and promises of endless boogie
Emotional distraction and crafty double speak
Where dogs are cats and
The poor are in fact very rich

Whirling

'Allah hu Allah hu'
chants the seeker after union
       in his dusty robes
He is whirling like a planet
around his inner sun - asking:

Who is the one
that will show the way beyond
the illusions of the self
Who is the one
that will show me His face

In another place a lover
whispers ' ya Allah '
in the throes
of another's ecstasy

Opaque yet iridescent
the country of the Soul
Where light clings to every instant
to every being - darkness
is a timeless blink away

A Karachi Wedding

The begums of the upper class
saunter up the path strewn
With red rose petals
Into the bright wedding tent
Their long dark hair trailing

Their postures weighed down
by necklaces of gold and gemstones

Even though it is past bedtime
a line of fine Pakistani crows
watches silently
for one of the begums
to drop

A Lahore Playground

I used to imagine I was a lucky man
Until the bomb blew away my child
We played upon the swings and we
Laughed running amongst the trees
Hide and seek and calling out his name
Until the bomb tore through the grounds
The laughter is a memory now
Swings are strange sculptures
Standing in a twisted landscape

Torn the age of tolerance
Like the charred pages of the Koran
Hanging from the scarred trees

And where are we friends
The ones who speak calmly and piously
Pointing heavenward to God's will
Can we not remember how to rage
Is it something stuck in our throat
That makes us so silent?

Sectarian times

Now the blood flows
It leaves its dark stain
On every town step
In coagulated streaks
But leaves no mark
Upon the memories of men

In these sectarian times
The veins are open now
The blood dance begins
History will not forgive
A rebellion that bears no fruit

A wingless dove…

In this land – the poets are all dead
And scavenging dogs
Control the shattered streets
But history will not bend
To the suffering of the earth
It will instead - redraw borders

Idols - no longer made of stone
They are taking shape
In the minds of men
And the call for life for a life
Rings from ancient minarets
These broken lines
These stranded narratives….

Yes the sands - are on the move
Yet the universal is lurking
Below the crashing roiling
Waves of history

Every year we tell each other
It's about to break through
To make of humanity - a unity
And yet here we stand
Staring at the ocean….

V

The Theft

In the middle of the night
Thieves broke into your house
And stole all your belongings
You shouted with happiness
And danced all night
Clutching the missing goblet!

A Dead Poet

A poet without a muse
        is a hapless fellow
Like a bedouin
        without a well

That is to say:
Open to the vultures -
Swift pickings
        under a remorseless sun
A sad ending
to a glorious future

Yet quite helpful
to the ecology of the whole

Invisible Things

A train of grey clouds across the orange sky
Two pink houses:
Transformed in the shimmering light

The street is deserted the houses empty
All the residents have all vanished
Was there an important broadcast?
Were they lifted to another dimension?

Then a man enters his front room
Bends slowly stiffly over a table
To tune what is surely an invisible radio
Perhaps he knows a secret that I don't

As I ponder these mysteries
A zephyr gently brushes my face
There is a tick-tock of a metronome
That is echoing my driven steps….
The husk of past the bugle of history
I must hurry:
For I am a man on a mission

Creators

We invented virtual reality….
We are projectors of reality
We are the interpreters of flames
We live in the house of doors
We tune the invisible keys
We strum the invisible strings
A thousand eclipses of the sun
    will never
        dim our bright arrows

Ode To My mother

It all started with a luminous memory
The poem came fully formed
But it was deleted by a restless finger…
I stare at the window across the street
The reflection must tell me something!
Instead it's the inert bricks that speak
There is no reflection here
      Go seek elsewhere!

Then I remember my mother yet again
My mother who was a poet of the heart
With a heart flowing with of compassion
With a soul that gazed calmly
      through soft direct eyes
She was a poet who jettisoned her poems
To reclaim some unknown ballast
In a journey upon an unknown ocean

Yes: that's how she saw things

I don't need to create idols
The world is overflowing with them
And they have colonized our dreams
Sneaking up at night disturbing peoples' sleep…
And what can I say about this caravan
We so fondly call life?
And how saddened am I by these bird cages
From which the birds have flown.

And there she was in my memory…
The God of Mirth dancing in her eyes

The Cave

It is in the nature of caves that
One day a stranger will appear
      It could be a messenger
Or someone who has lost his way
Or a mystic looking for company
      It could simply be you
Come to clean out an unruly tenant

In the cave
It is one day lost another gained

Then one day you see her – that Almadena
Almadena from the mysterious night
And sometimes - the luminous day
She was there alright -
As she was at the beginning
And surely will be at the end
You beckoned her to come in
But she turned and walked away:
To the empty deserts – to the icy North
To the deep forests - the trembling mountains

And you who live in the cave
Tired and broken and stiffened
Your time is different to hers
For she moves in an adjacent zone
But you knew that –

As she went her indifferent way
Carried away on an eddy of time
Leaving you alone – to build
Your ladder in the cave

A Special Case

You have it now friend!
It's the dance of the atoms
So give a thunderous applause!
Let the minstrels roam - the dancers dance
To drown out this endless discourse
Between a smug Idealist and a surly Atomist
It's being spread all over town -
And no one can sleep for their cries:
It is the seven dances in your Brain!
NO! NO!
It is the seven dimensions of Being!

(Somebody should lock them up)

There are many waves lapping
At the shores of your soul friend
Are you the Kosmos itself?
Are you the answer to a riddle?
Your vision is mighty - true and bold
Like spring flowers on the downs of heather
Friend your end will come
As it does to all - to all
It's the mystery code!
The journey!
The exit!

You are a special case yes – a live broadcast
In an infinite field of time and space
Strung between heaven and earth
And your bones ache for light
Like the lotus opening to the morning sun
So too you are open to the mystical sun
Without and within it is
Present time future time
Fused in this very moment – and therein
It's the secret code!
The life!
The exit!

A Rural Evening

You have said enough already –
All evening: a dialogue between the deaf
An outpouring of the empty to the empty

The wind is not your slave

The orchestra of evening birds
Is winding down to a grudging silence
The crows are settling for the night
The wheat is growing vivid green
The cane is dense ready to be cut
The snakes are all snugly curled up -
For it's a cold night in Cholistan.

There – a solitary *Koel's* mournful call
Above - the ever circling constellations
It is time to hippity-hop and jigidy-jig down
the old avenue guarded by eucalyptus trees

The Dialectic

A conversation is eternally in play
Between the little light we shine
And the big light that is occult
Between Being and the becoming

And if you are one of those who's
Mind's eye aperture does not register
The internal and subjective universe
Then consider the sheer exuberance
The sheer impersonality - of it all
Or the beauty that is given to us
Imbedded in the irredentist coral reefs
That we are impelled to navigate
In our lives - which are not just ours

We are petals unfurled
In the fury of some great fire
Oh what a game to which we awake
Born in the first light - of yes WONDER
We are of no fixed address
No GPS can triangulate us
We do not come with a postal code
We are spread all over the place
Yet to be sure we belong
To each other - at the very least

Handcuffed to a chain gang of seven billion

In this there is no mystical whimsy
For the mind loves the unknown
Like some proud Don Quixote
Forever tilting at the unknowable
And it is all too self-evident
That consciousness is imbedded
In every expression of Kosmos

A spectacular devolution!

All nouns are verbs on their way
To becoming nouns -
Frozen particularities of meaning
It is a self-actualizing universe – in the playground
Of Great Time and Great Space
Electricity is not just its appearance
The light not just it's shining
And Being not the figment of your brain
Or Mind your only resident….

Welcome To The World

An octave is but a note
In yet another octave
Nesting harmonies…
Everything celestial orbits
Some grander entity
Lock-step geometries / interlocking fields
And the gods are laughing for
Most of the cosmic matter / is missing
No doubt hiding in plain sight

Sun rays through your hat
Soul rays through your heart
Welcome to the world
It is newly born

You may lose your love
But love will not lose you
It will find you in your corner
Huddled against the world
It will loosen your bow tie
And hang up your shirt
Welcome to the world
It is newly born

It is awaiting your decision
It is awaiting your sound -
So it can begin to live
So it can begin to roll like thunder
Or hurtle like an out-of-control train
Yes - you may lose your life
Yet life will not lose you
For the Kosmos is your very own

It is conducting a symphony
In the corridors of your bones

The Announcement

I am a frequent visitor to airports
Inevitably travelling from East to West
And then from West to East -
And on one such a day in a departure lounge
I was to hear this announcement:
There are poets who have never written a poem
There are poems which have never seen daylight
There are singers who have never sung
There are lovers who have never loved
There are saints who have never fainted
There are humanists without humanity
There are stranded angels without wings
There are energies looking for forms
And Ladies and Gentlemen listen up:
Please consider as you circumnavigate
This blue planet floating in a vast cosmos
Is there a thought without a thinker?
Is there a creation without a creator?

I stop at that very airport each year
Always hoping to catch another announcement
But there is nothing - only a yellow paper moon
Hanging against the sky-high windows

Leading me to believe there must be:
Announcements without announcers

The Metaphysical God:

Hello hello ! My dears hello!
This is your God speaking
I announce myself this way with some curiosity
As I emerge from my purdah
Unveiling an aspect of myself to your world
For I am a curious fellow - yes
Many humans maintain that I don't exist
As if existence in the human domain
Was some defining mode for God
Like your laws of physics or of harmonics

Hello my dears hello
I am your God and I give you my word
That I am a Curious Fellow
You call me by many names –as if
Names could somehow define my 'Being'
Flattery and insults are the same to me
I am beyond your affirmations and your denials
It is a truism that curiosity killed the cat
In my case curiosity spawned a Kosmos
For me there is no time - between the concept
And its creation
That is how it is with me

I gifted you creation's Algorithm
You who are contained within
The ring-pass-not of your world
You who are building the pyramid of knowledge
With your brain filters fully engaged
Remember to keep the corners straight
Your soul is a blue-print – not a promise
No amount of blood-letting will draw my attention
No need to refer to me as your Father
Or The Beloved of your visions
Think of me in terms of real-estate
Think of me as your Landlord
      If you must think of me at all
For I am beyond your conception yet
Within the compass of your imagination
Or to make even simpler: think of me as
The absolutely Absolute Everything
I must leave you now my dears
For I feel Mirth arising in my 'Being'
This Mirth is like a long distance build up
To what in your world is called an 'orgasm'
And if it builds and builds
To a full scale belly laugh
Then there will be no holding back

The BANG!

The Gift

I have a name yet I am not the name
I am not rooted in one place but many
Where ever I am / my head is elsewhere
Borders are a burden / imposed identities
I cross them often / with a smiling face
As if I belonged

I have left a part of me in each place
Residing in the left-luggage lock-up
And each return to a location
I have to redeem a piece of myself
With a magical token my mother long ago
Placed around my eleven-year-old neck
Not like a talisman but more like a key
The day she put me on a plane to London

And she gave me her parting advice:
Do not mix just with your own kind
Do not tamper with the dark side
The world is round everywhere
Everywhere there is longing
Everywhere there is belonging
You are a soul deep and kind
For you everything in due time
There is a Self that is constant
There is a truth that is bold...

And as I walk the streets of this city
I see her words as a gift - a key
That will forever adorn my neck

Postcard To My Son

The broken tree
The shattered night
The incendiary grief…

Since you left us
The Earth has travelled
Thirteen billion miles
But we
Have not moved an inch

Alive
The memory of you
In a quiet place
Like a tiny fluttering bird
In the palm of a hand
And your existence
Is a gentle harmony
Deep in our hearts

The old peepal tree
In the garden now shades
Our solitude

The Witness

When the game is won
When the form is cast
And the prophesy spun
Who
Will call your name

When the deed is done
When the night is come
And the shadow is gone
Who will witness
The game

When sorrow is spent
And the magic woven
And the silk is spun
Who will recall
Your fame

Who will decipher
The smoking skid marks left
By the life
That you so nobly claim

Aknowledgment

I am most grateful to my friend and publisher
Franc Roddam, for this collection would not have
seen the light of day without his persistent and
enthusiastic encouragement and guidance.

My thanks go to the poet Tim Murphy
and Zayn Khan, Suzanne Khan and Leila Ansari
for their valued comments and suggestions, and to
other family and friends who provided a steady flow
of supportive energy.